NORE



# The Final Frontier

## Stories by
## Sue Hines, David Hill and
## Marianne de Pierres

Ginn

Ginn is a registered trademark of Harcourt Education Ltd.

Linacre House, Jordan Hill, Oxford, OX2 8DP
a division of Harcourt Education Ltd

**Visit www.myprimary.co.uk to see a chart showing you all the Pocket Reads programme information you will need.**



From the Spinouts project developed by Paul Collins and Meredith Costain.



08 07 06 05
10 9 8 7 6 5 4 3 2

ISBN 0602 243211 / 978 0602 243210

Nuts! illustrated by Andrew Plant
The White Rooms illustrated by Kevin Burgemeestre
Mig's Choosing illustrated by Jiri Tibor Novak

Cover illustration by Marc McBride

Designed by Carolyn Gibson

Repro by Digital Imaging, Glasgow

Printed and bound in China through Phoenix Offset

# CONTENTS

## About Sue Hines

Sue Hines writes to stay sane, and to avoid housework and televised sport. She shares her house with a son, two cats and various spiders.

## About the story

"This was going to be a nice story about two lonely children whose heroic dad gave them great presents, but somehow it turned into something creepy and sinister. I like the way stories do that sometimes. They take on a life of their own and drag you along for the ride."

Sue Hines

# Nuts!

by Sue Hines

When Commander Vigo's children grew old enough to know better, they stopped crying every time he left on a mission. Their father always brought back something for them that would make the fatherless months worthwhile.

So far he'd brought back presents that made all their friends horribly envious. The envy helped make up for all the times Little Vigo and Stella were alone in the house with only the android servants for company.

Commander Vigo of the IMC Starfleet had a very important job – exploring the universe and visiting the Interworld Mining Company's far-flung settlements. Stella and Little Vigo never let their friends forget it. Especially Jake Tunnelman, whose father's immense wealth came from several mines in poor regions of the homeworld. Jake had an enormous room for all his fancy gadgets and computer games, but everything in *his* room came from the homeworld. The Tunnelman empire was *strictly* homeworld, as Little Vigo kept reminding Jake with a superior smirk.

On the day of Commander Vigo's latest return, the children could hardly contain their excitement as they waited in the reception area at the transit station.

Their father looked different, somehow. Perhaps it was the haunted look in his eyes, or perhaps he was not as upright as they remembered. He looked very, very hungry.

"Dad! What happened to you?" Little Vigo's voice echoed with distaste. His heroic father looked distinctly unheroic.

"I'm just tired, son. There was some trouble in the outer quadrant of Sector Seven, but it's all under control now."

"Stupid aliens," sniffed Little Vigo. "When will they realise they can't fight the IMC?"

Commander Vigo ruffled his son's hair. "An uncivilised lot like that? It didn't take long to fix things. Now, kiddies, wait till you see what I brought back for you!"

The nut from the small, rebellious planet in Sector Seven was beautiful. Its pearly shell shimmered and quivered in the light, and gave off a cool silvery glow when Commander Vigo turned out the light.

"Ready?" he said, his hands shaking as he placed the nut into the nutcracker.

The children held their breath. Their father was going to destroy the present he had brought them!

As the glowing shell shattered, a small, satisfied sigh escaped from the nut, and a marvellous aroma, somewhere between summer rain and baking bread, filled the

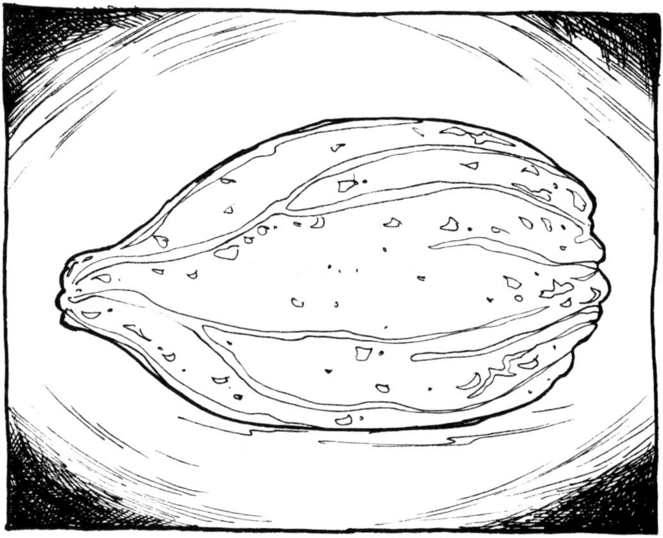

children's nostrils. Little Vigo snatched up the small green nut and put it to his lips.

"Can I, Dad? Is it safe?"

Commander Vigo's eyes glowed like black pearls, and he grinned slowly.

"Go ahead, son. It's the most delicious thing you'll ever eat."

"Dad, Dad!" squealed Stella, pointing at the shell fragments on the table. They were humming with a strange energy. Every single fragment swelled and hummed with a strange life force, and in no time at all a new nut sat in the place of each fragment, quivering like a jewel.

Commander Vigo showed all his teeth, picked up one of the new nuts and cracked it. Greedily stuffing the fleshy green nut between his lips, he chewed rapidly. An expression of relief washed over his features. From the fragments of his nutshell, another handful of nuts grew, and Commander Vigo smashed them hungrily, pushing the nuts into his mouth.

"Brilliant, isn't it?" he said, spraying tiny crumbs over his children. "A renewable food source that's delicious, nutritious and *free*! Just think, you can sell the shelled product at any price you like, and have an unending source of wealth in the nutshells!"

His voice was heavy, his words a little slurred. "This is going to change the world as we know it. If you thought we were rich before, you just wait till Darisian nut-butter hits the shelves!"

Bel Ma'an smiled at her mother. "Please tell me the story again."

When Bel Na'arya spoke of the glorious revolution that would free Daris from the evil grasp of the Interworld Mining Company, her little daughter stopped seeing the destruction of her planet, and saw hope instead.

Since long before Ma'an was born, enormous laser cutters had been hacking gigantic slices from the surface of her planet. Now almost nothing grew on Daris, because the goodness from much of the surface of the planet had been stolen by the machines of the IMC. Darisian minerals made an excellent and cheap fuel for the company's starships.

The people of Daris were starving and dying. Ma'an could not remember a time when she had eaten anything apart from a stringy but nutritious fruit that grew in poor soil and tasted like old socks, and slimy marine algae that squirmed all the way down her throat. She knew better than to eat the parasitic ma'nna nuts that thrived in the wastelands left by the IMC's laser cutters, no matter how hungry she became.

"Once upon a time," Bel Na'arya began, "long before the IMC enslaved us, Daris was a beautiful world. You cannot imagine how things grew and covered the surface of our planet. All around there was colour and ripeness that grew from the goodness within the earth. When I was a girl, my skin was firm and smooth, like the skin of all the old Darisians. It was nothing like this cracked and scaly armour we all have now. That is a sign of our poor diet, and marks us as slaves.

"One day a starship of the IMC came to us. We were fascinated by these beings from the sky. They brought gifts and made a show of befriending us, and we agreed to share our prosperity with them. Fools!

"But these invaders do not know how to share. They only know how to take. In no time, their machines began cutting pieces of Daris away, processing the surface of our lovely planet to make fuel for their ships. When our new crops failed and our food supply hit critical levels, they had us right where they wanted us."

The skinny, scaly little girl squirmed in her ragged clothes. She knew what was coming next.

"But Darisians are a proud people. Hunger and enslavement have not destroyed our spirit, and we have learned a few tricks of our own from the IMC."

"Tricks!" crowed Ma'an, her voice quivering.

Na'arya nodded. "Oh yes," she said, with a kind of music in her voice. "We learned that the invaders will take anything, if they think it has value, or they can profit from it. After many dangerous secret meetings, held in the darkness underground, a group of us put our liberation plan into action."

It was an ingenious plan. A small group of Darisians, including Bel Na'arya, began harvesting the ma'nna nuts from the wastelands in secret. They made a clever show of creating a black market for the nuts.

Secret pamphlets advertised them as "delicious, nutritious – the answer to Darisian hunger!" IMC spies "discovered" this secret commerce, as they were meant to, and informed Commander Vigo immediately. He couldn't get his starship there fast enough, and there were some uncomfortable and dangerous moments when the Darisian "merchants" pretended to fight for their nut crops.

Of course, the IMC won, as it always did, and the puny, scaly Darisians wept and wailed and tried to hide their glee as Commander Vigo took a shipload of ma'nna nuts back to his world.

What Commander Vigo didn't know was that no Darisian in her right mind would actually crack or eat the highly addictive ma'nna. One taste was enough to enslave the mind, and create an insatiable hunger for more ma'nna nuts. A hunger that would lead to madness and worse.

Stella found something about her father's frenzied nut-cracking distasteful, and resisted the urge to eat any of the Darisian nuts. Now she watched with growing horror as her world changed.

Commander Vigo never went to work any more, and the IMC Starfleet languished while its crews feasted on Darisian ma'nna nuts. The Commander sat with an ever-growing pile of nuts before him, cracking each one and shovelling the flesh into his waiting mouth. He was becoming as round as a Darisian nut himself. He sweated profusely, and his skin seemed to have taken on a pearly sheen.

Stella hadn't seen Little Vigo for days, since he had sneaked out with a Darisian nut.

"Jake Tunnelman's got a laser grinder," he'd confided, his voice squeaky with excitement. "I reckon he'll grind this baby to powder. Do you know how many new nuts we'll get from that? I'll make a killing at school, although I suppose I'll have to cut Jake in."

Stella had given up trying to get any sense out of anybody – only the android servants seemed immune to the lure of the Darisian nuts, and they weren't worth talking to anyway. They weren't even human, for goodness' sake. Everybody else wore a haunted expression that only faded when fed with Darisian nuts. It was horrible.

"Mother, what do you suppose is happening on Commander Vigo's world right now?" mused Bel Ma'an, her skin already starting to lose its scaly appearance.

"Well, darling, you know ma'nna is parasitic, don't you? When the number of parasites becomes too great, and there is a danger that the hosts will be unable to keep feeding them, the host's body undergoes a rather dramatic change."

Stella screamed when she heard the explosion from her father's study, and the inhuman cry that accompanied it. What had happened to her father? She huddled on a sofa, too afraid to investigate, and cried with relief when Commander Vigo dashed out of his study looking for a new supply of Darisian nuts.

"Dad, you're OK!" she gasped, but the words froze on her lips. From the study came another Commander Vigo, and another, and another. The thundering of their boots threatened to drown out their desperate cries.

"Nuts! Nuts! More nuts!"

## About David Hill

David Hill lives in New Zealand. He has been a teacher, a soldier and a driver, but now he writes full-time. He likes walking, reading, astronomy, and cheering for New Zealand's rugby team.

## About the story

"I remember how, when I was a lot younger, my mates and I were always pretending to be astronauts and space heroes. And when I wasn't quite so young, I still pretended such things – though I never told anyone! Plus I remember how nobody at any age seems to like visiting those silent, scary places which I've called ... The White Rooms."

David Hill

# The White Rooms

**by David Hill**

The control panel was dead. No lights flickered. No screens glowed.

Cosmonaut Ffilc knew what the sudden instrument failure meant. Any minute now, the Aliens and the Hunters would be here.

He checked the control panel one last time, trying every backup system. The Proton Burner. The Warp Drive Emergency Cut-In. The Play Station. No use.

How long since Mission Control had spoken to him? How long since the sound of a friendly voice? Could be hours. Could be days.

Ffilc thought of another voice, and shuddered. It was the voice of his best friend, Evad, calling just before the Aliens and their

Hunters reached him, too. "They're waiting for me, Ffilc," Evad had whispered. "I ... I have to go."

"Take the injection, Evad!" Ffilc told him. "You – you won't feel things so much if you do." But Evad had gone.

Soon Ffilc would be gone, too. He sat totally still now, while his starship hung in the black emptiness of space.

Out there, the temperature was 267 degrees below zero. If anyone stepped outside, their blood would immediately freeze into tiny icy splinters.

Any people that happened to would be lucky, Ffilc thought grimly. At least they wouldn't have to face the Aliens and the Hunters.

Ffilc held his breath suddenly. Somewhere outside the cabin he heard an electric motor whining and sucking. It stopped, whined and sucked again, then faded into silence.

That was it, Ffilc knew. The Aliens were closing down all the machines. The Nintendo – yes, even the Nintendo would be stopped. Soon the Aliens would come for him, taking him away.

Away to the White Rooms.

Ffilc knew about the White Rooms. All cosmonauts knew about them. Only the very lucky would escape them.

It was strange how quiet his starship became, as the support networks failed one by one.

Ffilc had realised what was happening as soon as the rumble of the great drive engines died away inside his head. It was a total systems breakdown, a breakdown that the Aliens had somehow planned. The Aliens thought of everything.

The ship vibrated suddenly. Ffilc turned again to the control panel, but still no lights flashed.

Maybe he was going to be lucky, and be pulled into a Black Hole? Then the enormous gravity of the collapsed star inside the Black Hole would stretch the starship and him into spaghetti. Maybe when he was inside the Black Hole, he'd be roasted by trapped starlight and fried by nuclear radiation? Then he'd be sucked into the middle of the hole –

where all matter was squashed into tiny atoms – and spat out the other side like a mouthful of muesli into a different universe. It would be better than being taken by the Aliens to the White Rooms.

He listened again. He thought he'd heard the low growl of a Hunter. He pictured the beast searching for him, fangs and claws bared as it tried to pick up his scent. Its Alien masters would be close behind.

Ffilc imagined what was outside his cabin. There would be blackness, the glitter of distant stars and the glow of far-off galaxies. And there would be the slow drift of dust from exploding stars.

Millions of years from now, that dust might float closer together, getting thicker and thicker, heating up under its own gravity till another star burst into fire, giving light and warmth and life to the planets around it. Ffilc hoped that any creatures on those planets would never have to face the Aliens and their White Rooms.

They were nearly there now. Ffilc knew it. That vibration a few minutes ago had told him.

They were getting ready for him. Soon they and the Hunters would come. He had an hour. No, less than an hour. Then he would have to face the pain, and the machines of the White Rooms.

Ffilc rose, and began pacing backwards and forwards across the pilot's cabin. In his mind, he went over the escape plans that he and Evad had talked about. The sudden dive for cover into the boiling clouds of Venus or the icy craters of the Moon? No use – the Aliens would simply wait and starve him out. Putting on his space-suit and blasting himself out into the darkness of space? They could hunt him there, too.

Cosmonaut Ffilc thought of his friend Evad once more, and swallowed. He tried the radio again, flicking from channel to channel. Mission Control stayed silent. Yes, thought Ffilc. That dying whine of the electric motor had been the sign that the real horror would come soon.

He checked his emergency compartments. His space-suit was useless, anyway. It was torn and ripped where the claws of the Lirg tribe had pierced it, while Evad and he had fought them off in one of the many battles they'd shared long ago.

The food lockers were empty. Even the last chocolate was gone. Ffilc shook his head. He shouldn't be thinking about chocolate at a time like this. But he couldn't help it – after all, he was a cosmonaut.

He sat, and let his hands drift across the switches and dials that had served Evad and him so well in the past. His mind turned again to the Aliens. To get what they wanted when they brought a cosmonaut into the White Rooms, they used something called the Chair of Pain. Great Jupiter! What creatures could invent such a thing? Even the Hunters fled from it.

Ffilc pushed his own chair back from the control panel. He gazed around him. The star charts, the computer, the wall lights, the chart of Ten Tasty Ways to Barbecue a Martian Xol-Bug – nothing could help him now.

Again, Ffilc thought of what might have been. If only he'd applied for a job polishing the nuclear reactors on a ten-year trip to Alpha Centauri. Or volunteered to test sunglasses by diving into the 15-million-degree centre of the Sun. If only he hadn't laughed at Evad's plans for a Hamburger Take-away Joint orbiting between Mars and Jupiter. But it was too late for any of that.

He froze. A cold finger seemed to touch his spine. Had he heard ...? No.

Yes. It was there, all right. The soft pad and low growl of a Hunter, just outside his cabin.

Then Ffilc jerked again, as a motor fired, caught, and began to hum. The Aliens were bringing one of their transporters into position. Very soon he would be strapped inside it, a helpless captive on his way to the White Rooms.

Maybe the Aliens wouldn't find him! If he stayed very still, maybe they would pass by his cabin?

No – a thudding, banging noise started up outside the cabin door. The Aliens had found him. He'd known they would. The Aliens were too clever and powerful. Their Hunters were too keen-eyed.

They always got you in the end.

Ffilc drew another deep breath. He stared around the walls again. *Why can't they just leave us alone?* he thought. But the Aliens and their white-clad allies never left anyone alone. Sooner or later, it was everyone's turn. Every cosmonaut had to suffer, while the Aliens bent over the Chair of Pain, or cackled and hissed on the padded benches.

The banging came again. It was louder now.

It was his own fault, Ffilc realised. He should never have admitted that he'd discovered a personal Black Hole. The Aliens hated Black Holes. They searched them out, then destroyed them with huge drills and blasters.

More banging. The flight compartment door swung open. Ffilc watched, mouth dry and heart thudding.

A shadow fell across the cabin floor, and a Hunter entered. Its eyes blazed at Ffilc. Its jaws opened, and he saw white fangs as it began moving towards him.

Towering behind the Hunter, another shape appeared. The first Alien stood there, staring at Ffilc.

*Incredible how the Aliens look so much like us*, Ffilc managed to think. All part of their hideous plan to fool and capture cosmonauts.

The Hunter stopped and crouched in front of him. Ffilc stared past it, at the Alien. The cold finger touched his spine again. How would the pain begin? What would be the words that started it?

He knew it was no use, but he spoke to the Alien in its own language. He spoke the one word that might somehow strike its cruel heart and keep him from the Chair of Pain and the White Rooms.

"Maarrmm?" he croaked.

The Alien's cruel mouth opened. It pushed past the crouching Hunter, and its voice came.

"Cliff? I – oh, get out of the way, Puss! Aren't you ready, son? I told you we'd go when I'd finished the vacuuming. Dad's waiting in the car – didn't you hear him? You can't stay here playing your space games. You can email Dave when you get back – you two and your funny backward-spelt names! Hurry up, dear, or you'll be late for the dentist!"

## About Marianne de Pierres

Marianne de Pierres lives in Australia with her husband, three sons and any passing koalas. She has the best fun writing stories for children but sometimes she gets very serious and writes novels for adults as well. Visit Marianne's website at www.mariannedepierres.com.

## About the story

"The idea for this story popped into my head when I wondered what it would be like to ride motorbikes in a fantasy land. Happy endings are cool, too."

Marianne de Pierres

# Mig's Choosing

**by Marianne de Pierres**

The Rat towered over me, his whiskers quivering. "You're gonna eat my dust on Saturday, Choom."

"His name's Chum," said my sister Terga, fiercely.

Rat looked at us doubtfully, scratching his furry face. Then his eyes lit like a glow worm. "Like dog food!" He swung around to his mates, Clueless and Tommo. "The little runt's named after dog food!"

He laughed – so Clueless and Tommo laughed too. They sauntered off like three whooping mutant hyenas.

"See you on the dunes!" I shouted angrily at their backs.

They laughed louder.

On Saturday I was riding my hover bike in a desert race. The same one as The Rat and his hyenas.

Everybody would "eat dust". That's what hover bike Enduro is about! Noise and dust! Or if you were really lucky and the race fell during the three moons (which meant rainstorms) – *slosh*!

But The Rat had meant "eat my dust" as an insult; that I'd finish the race behind him. Only

The Rat was wrong. This was my year. I was going to win my age category.

You see, there was a special prize. Once every ten years Mig the famous space captain landed on our planet and chose an apprentice. You had to be a boy between the ages of ten and twelve.

This year was my only chance!

Saturday morning dawned hot and fine, like most other days here. Terga helped me fuel the bike from a fuel tree.

"I'm going to win," I said.

She stared at me, her bright green eyes slanted under her veil. "What about The Rat?"

I made a rude sound. "Rat. Splat!"

She bowed her head quickly. "If Mig chooses you, we'll be separated forever."

"Not forever," I said softly. "I'll send you money when I can. I'll come back."

Terga turned away. But I could hear her voice quiver. "No you won't."

Terga and I lived in a floating tent on the edge of Achmet's Oasis. We had never known our parents. It had been just the two of us ever since old Granna died.

We divided the chores. Terga fixed servant robots for the rich tent owners. (She'd made my bike from cast-off bits of robot. Terga loved to tinker!) I cooked the meals and cleaned, and painted portraits in the market.

We made enough to eat. Most of the time. When we didn't, we'd lie in bed at night and I'd make up stories to distract us from our rumbling bellies. My stories were always about being chosen as Mig's apprentice. And how one day I would come and rescue Terga. We'd fly into space together and become famous.

The bike race was the most important thing that happened in the Oasis all year. When Mig was choosing an apprentice, it was ten times as important. Achmet's would be crowded. The competition would be tough – to be taken on by Mig meant seeing the universe, good food and new clothes – but I was ready.

Terga rode the bike with me to the starting line. The crowds swelled around us like dust in a sandstorm.

She gave me a quick, fierce hug. "Be swift," she said.

"I thought you didn't want me to win?" I asked, surprised.

Her green eyes filled with tears. "I do. I do. It's the only way out. I can't explain. But you must win. Promise me?"

I tugged on her veil and grinned. "See you at the finishing line."

She jumped lightly onto the ground and disappeared into the crowd.

I scanned the line of bikes. Clueless hovered up on my right side. Tommo was three or four away. About ten entries in all, I reckoned. But where was The Rat?

I checked over my fuel levels and tweaked the throttle ready for a fast start. A noise like a night-camel roar startled me. A bike nosed into place on my left. It was black with white tusks sticking out of each side. The Rat's furry face leered out.

"Ready to be dusted, dog chow?"

I didn't answer. Instead I practised breathing slowly to relax. The way old

Granna had taught me. But out of the corner of my eye, I could see The Rat's long whiskers quivering.

Then trumpets blared aloud as Mig's orbital transit car descended from the sky. I searched for Terga but I couldn't see her. Her voice echoed in my head.

*You must win! It's the only way out.*

The bikes whined as their riders held them in check. My skin prickled at the sound.

Mig stepped dramatically down a set of stairs that hung from the belly of his car. His cloak flowed about him like a bat's wings. His beard fell below his waist.

Without speaking, he waved the starter's flag.

I stomped on the throttle with all my might. The line of machines blurred as I shot away. I found that I was holding my breath.

Three or four bikes crowded on my right. Clueless and Tommo would be two of them. To my left, and a length in front, was The Rat. I could see the white tusks grinning back at me.

I twitched my throttle as we rounded sand dunes, cornering faster than anyone else. Except The Rat. Quickly the race strung out. Five left for dead. Three close behind me, and two in front.

*Two??*

I swerved left to get out of The Rat's dust and to get a better look.

Sure enough, a length in front of The Rat was another bike. Sleek and small and emerald green.

Whose?

I didn't have time to wonder. The Rat cut across me and crunched my bike's nose with his tusks. Tommo shoved me from behind. I spun like a coin; out of control.

*You must win!* Terga's words urged me on. I yanked the wheel across with all my might, hauling myself back on course.

By the second lap, I'd caught up with The Rat again.

I was ready for him this time. I nosed closer, tempting him. He swung his tail across to bounce me. I braked and he missed me. This time it was The Rat who spun away into the sand.

"Eat *my* dust!" I thought, grinning. Half a lap to go. He'd never catch up.

That left only one to beat; the emerald bike.

As we soared over the last set of dunes, I pushed my bike to its limit. It wobbled and thrashed. But I rode it like a wild night-camel.

The finish line came into sight and I squeezed the last life out of my bike. With a groan it threw itself alongside the emerald machine and we flashed past the finish together.

"Dead heat! Dead heat! Dead heat!" the crowd screamed as I slowed and limped my bike back.

With an elegant wave Mig called us to his hovering stairway. I slid back the bike's hood and waited, trembling. Surely there couldn't be two winners? I wished Terga were with me. But I couldn't see her in the press of the crowd.

Then Mig spoke and the crowd hushed. "My instruments tell me that the race is a dead heat. This has never happened before. I will know the names of the two contestants."

I removed my goggles and spoke loudly and clearly. "My name is Chum. An orphan of Achmet's Oasis. My greatest wish is to be Mig's apprentice."

Mig nodded his approval.

He and I turned to look at the emerald bike.

The driver removed his goggles slowly, as though shy, his back to me. His hair was cut short and ragged. His voice higher-pitched than mine, and quiet. So quiet, I strained to catch it.

"My name is Ches, from Achmet's Outland. I too have the same wish."

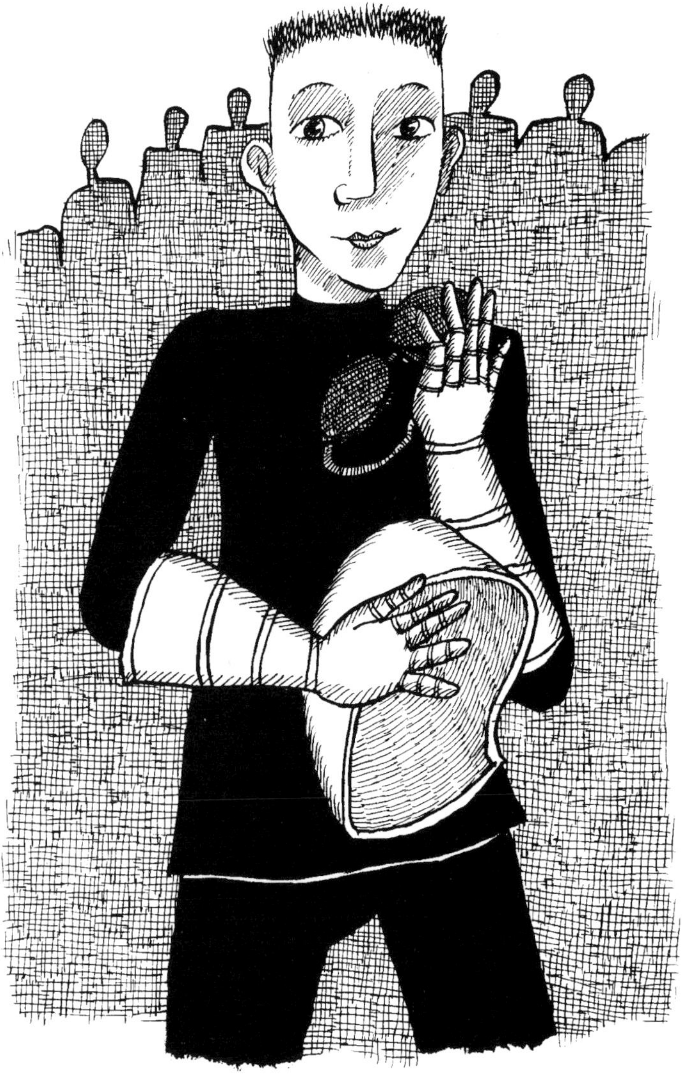

*An outlander?* No wonder I didn't know him. Outlanders seldom came to the Oasis.

Mig stared hard at Ches for a long moment, as if making a decision. Then he beamed out upon the crowds.

"Today will be remembered as 'Mig's Twin Choosing'. A special day in history, when Mig accepted two apprentices." He clapped his hands. "Now, Ches and Chum, cross palms. Then let us leave, there is much to learn."

I nudged my bike closer to do as Mig had bidden. Relief swamped me: I had been chosen. And terrible sadness: I would not even get to say goodbye to Terga.

As I met Ches's eyes, my own were filled with tears that I couldn't stop.

A small, warm hand squeezed mine. "I told you that you had to win," Ches said with a whisper.

I blinked and stared with surprise into green eyes I knew better than my own. They were set in a face so different with short, ragged hair and boys' clothes. A face that meant no sad goodbyes!

Terga's!